MW01010791

TERRORIST
DOSSIERS

AGAINST ALL ODDS

Counterterrorist HOSTAGE RESCUES

Samuel M. KATZ

Lerner Publications Company/Minneapolis

To the victims of terror
—SMK

Publisher's Note: The information in this book was current at the time of publication. However, the
publisher is aware that news involving current events dates quickly. Please refer to the websites on
pages 68–69 for places to go to obtain up-to-date information.

Lerner Publications Company
A division of Lerner Publishing Group
241 First Avenue North
Minneapolis, Minnesota U.S.A.

Website address: www.lernerbooks.com

Library of Congress Cataloging-in-Publication Data

Katz, Samuel M., 1963–
    Against all odds : counterterrorist hostage rescues / by Samuel M. Katz.
        p.   cm. — (Terrorist dossiers)
    Includes bibliographical references and index.
    ISBN: 0–8225–1567–9 (lib. bdg. : alk. paper)
    1. Hostages—Case studies. 2. Rescues—Case studies. 3. Police—Special weapons and tactics
units—Case studies. I. Title. II. Series.
HV8058.K38 2005
363.32—dc22   2004006215

Manufactured in the United States of America
1 2 3 4 5 6 – DP – 10 09 08 07 06 05

CONTENTS

INTRODUCTION

The operator's armor-covered body was in the prone position, ready to leap forward as soon as the door had been breached. Adrenaline pumped through his limbs. He tightly clutched his MP5 submachine gun, focusing his energies on getting inside the door on a hostage-rescue operation. He went through his mental checklist, analyzing the intelligence he had been briefed on, reviewing the scenario he had prepared for.

Questions battered his mind as he stayed in his quiet pose. What was going on behind the doors he was about to burst through? Were the hostages being beaten and tortured? How were the female hostages?

The operator didn't have long to wait. Courtesy of the secure communications system worn inside his protective helmet, he learned that an explosive was to go off in exactly twenty seconds. The explosion blew the heavy metal doors off their frames in a thunderous blast that created a cloud of smoke and debris. Gunfire erupted from the two side rooms. The operator moved quickly through the fragments and acrid black smoke, firing his MP5 to terminate any terrorist target. He tried to shut out the vision of men and women, some bound and gagged, lying on the floor writhing in fear and agony. The operator's first instinct was to help the hostages, but that would come next. The most pressing business at hand was to make sure any terrorist in the building was dead or in handcuffs. The operator moved quickly into the first floor, clearing room after room.

More than twenty operators in three teams swarmed into the location from a variety of angles. The operator's assault team had cleared and secured the first floor. A second team had raced into the location through a second-floor bedroom window. A third team had landed via helicopter atop the roof. A support team of operators and medics helped evacuate the dozen or so captives who had been held in the now-liberated building. Clearing the two-story structure had taken ninety seconds.

The operator emerged from the building drenched in his own sweat. He unfastened the Velcro strip that secured his body armor to his torso and removed his armored kneepads. Slinging his MP5 across his shoulder, the

Operators train in Kevlar body armor.

operator sat down and watched as intelligence agents and emergency medical personnel took care of relieved hostages.

He was about to remove his helmet when the unit commander ordered him on his feet. "Get your gear back on," the operator was told, "the assault wasn't perfect. We are going to do it again from the top!"

For years, hostage-rescue operations have personified counterterrorism. This cruel drama is acted out in grueling slow motion. Politicians, the media, and the negotiators are all members of the cast. But the true superstars are the counterterrorist operators who burst through the doors or windows of buses, trains, planes, and buildings. Their skills, their training, their courage, and their gear are all factors that determine if the hostages live or perish. Under intense pressure and with the highest odds at stake, these professional soldiers and police officers must perform and get it right. One false move can result in bloody failure.

Counterterrorism and hostage rescue are not clear-cut sciences. Situations fluctuate fast. Adaptation, improvisation, and outside-the-box thinking are factors that determine if a rescue is going to succeed.

Each of the hostage rescues chronicled in this book carried the reality that the odds were stacked against success and a happy ending. Each rescue profiles people who refused to give up simply because the challenge seemed impossible.

TERRORIST DOSSIERS

WHO'S WHO AND WHAT'S WHAT

Black September Organization: a terrorist group founded in 1971 and named after September 1970 attacks by Jordanian forces on Palestinian refugee camps in Jordan

Captain Rifa'at: the leader of the terrorist team that took over Sabena Airlines Flight 571 in 1972

commando: a soldier specially trained to carry out raids

Ehud Barak: a highly decorated officer in the Israeli army who led an elite commando unit of the Sayeret Mat'kal. He would later become prime minister of Israel.

Idi Amin Dada: ruler of Uganda from 1971 to 1979. He called for the destruction of Israel and killed or exiled Ugandans who opposed his policies.

Islam: a religion founded on the Arabian Peninsula in the seventh century A.D. by the prophet Muhammad. Those who practice Islam are called Muslims.

Israel: a Middle Eastern country formed in 1948 as a Jewish homeland. Citizens of Israel are known as Israelis, and the country's official language is Hebrew. Many Jews and Palestinians believe both groups have historical rights to the region that includes Israel.

Israel Defense Forces (IDF): Israel's primary security and military organization

Munich Olympic Massacre: the capture and later execution of eleven Israeli athletes at the Summer Olympic Games in 1972 by Black September. The failed response to the crisis is considered a turning point in counterterrorism.

Palestine Liberation Organization (PLO): a group founded in 1964 to represent Palestinian interests. It is regarded by some as a terrorist organization.

Palestinian: an Arab native to the historically disputed region that includes the modern country of Israel

Popular Front for the Liberation of Palestine (PFLP): a terrorist group founded in late 1967 by Dr. George Habash

Red Army Faction (RAF): a West German terrorist group most active in the late 1960s and 1970s

Sayeret Mat'kal: the elite, counterterrorist unit of the IDF. Created in 1957, it is charged with intelligence gathering deep behind enemy lines.

special operations: activities, mostly in secret, conducted by special forces for particular military or political purposes

United Nations: formed in 1945, an organization of nations that works for world peace and security

Yonatan "Yoni" Netanyahu: a U.S.-born commando leader of Israel's Sayeret Mat'kal. He led the raid at Entebbe in 1976 but was killed during the fighting.

RESCUES BY THE SAYERET MAT'KAL OF ISRAEL

On November 29, 1947, the United Nations (UN) voted to split the ancient land of Palestine into two independent states—one Jewish, the other Arab. The Jews of Palestine welcomed the proposal and the promise of a state in their ancient homeland. Native Palestinians and neighboring Arab states vehemently opposed the plan.

Despite the disagreement, the Jewish State of Israel was declared on May 14, 1948. War soon followed, with Arab troops invading the new nation. Israeli troops counterattacked, eventually gaining more territory than Israel had been granted under the UN plan. Thousands of Palestinians chose to go to refugee camps in Jordan and elsewhere rather than to live within Israel's borders.

These events and later wars steadily escalated tensions between Israelis and Palestinians over the next two decades. Hit-and-run attacks by Palestinian groups became common. But these unorganized efforts frustrated many Palestinians who wanted a homeland immediately, at any

In the 1950s, Palestinian hit-and-run attack toppled an Israeli truck filled with food.

cost. Terrorist organizations emerged that were dedicated to taking the struggle to new levels of violence.

In September 1970, as international outcry against Palestinian terrorism grew, Jordanian forces attempted to purge Palestinian terrorist guerrilla forces from Jordanian refugee camps. The conflict that followed was bloody. More than 25,000 people were killed during the month-long fighting. The Jordanian government succeeded in expelling the Palestinian guerrilla forces, which ended up in Lebanon and Syria. The Palestine Liberation Organization (PLO) vowed revenge against Jordan and Israel. It created the Black September Organization, a covert terrorist entity whose operations were intended to grab the world's attention with the barrel of an AK-47 assault rifle.

Europe's liberal immigration and travel policies gave the organization the opportunity to make its statement.

Palestinian guerrillas *(above)* battled Jordanian troops in September 1970.

Brussels, the capital of Belgium and one of Black September's main European hubs, would be the starting point.

| OPERATION ISOTOPE 1, MAY 8–9, 1972 |

The long line of passengers moved slowly at the gate of Brussels International Airport in Belgium to board Sabena Flight 571 on the afternoon of May 8, 1972. The Boeing 707's flight was supposed to take less than five hours to reach Israel. The roughly one hundred passengers struggled with their carry-on luggage and duty-free purchases as they boarded the aircraft. Intermingled within the long line of passengers were four Palestinians—two men and two women, all members of Black September. The two men carefully scrutinized the passengers and examined the shiny jet. The two young women flirted with the machine-gun toting airport security officers.

The plane took off without incident and soared to cruising altitude. As the plane flew southeastward toward Israel, the four Palestinians calmly emerged from their seats and moved toward the cockpit. They took up strategic positions throughout the aircraft.

THE HIJACKING

On a signal, they removed their concealed weapons, entered the cockpit, and took control of the 707. The Palestinian commander of the operation was Ali Taha Abu Saneina, a legend within the ranks of the Palestinian revolutionary movement, who was known simply as Captain Rifa'at.

Over the intercom, Captain Rifa'at announced that the aircraft had been seized in the name of Palestine. Instead of diverting the airliner to Lebanon, Syria, or Jordan, as past terrorists had done, he told the frightened passengers that they were heading to Israel's Lod Airport. Black September was daring the mighty Israel Defense Forces (IDF) to respond.

The members of Sayeret Mat'kal—the covert intelligence-gathering force—were the IDF's elite. They were given the job of rescuing the hostages and apprehending or eliminating the terrorists.

FIRST STEPS

Upon landing at Lod Airport, Flight 571 was diverted to a remote area where it was surrounded by hundreds of khaki-uniformed members of the national border police. They trained their weapons on the aircraft, not knowing what the terrorists' plans were. Yet Rifa'at, calm and cool, knew how to play the game. Hours into the ordeal, he released his demands to Israeli negotiators, who had been trying in vain to establish communications with the hijackers.

Captain Reginald Levy, the skipper of the hijacked craft, read Rifa'at's demands at the barrel of a 9mm pistol. More than three hundred Palestinian

Israeli border guards surround the hijacked Sabena Airlines plane *(in the background)* at Lod Airport.

terrorists were to be released in less than twenty-four hours and brought to the tarmac at Lod. If Captain Rifa'at's demands were not met, the hostages would be executed.

Darkness fell over Lod at around 7:00 P.M. on May 8. Major General Aharon Yariv, the head of military intelligence, was personally conducting the tense negotiations over a radio set.

As Major General Yariv embarked on his Herculean task, Lieutenant Colonel Ehud Barak and his Sayeret Mat'kal unit of commandos arrived at the airport. Barak knew that Captain Rifa'at's clock was ticking.

TRULY WIRED

In the 1970s and 1980s, the delicate art of negotiations between hostage takers and government officials was conducted through radio handsets, messengers, and even hand signals. The hijackers used their instincts to judge the truth of the information they received. The negotiators, on the other hand, had far greater secrecy. Before mobile phones, negotiators didn't have to worry that a terrorist on the ground could discreetly report the movement of rescue forces. The days of a negotiator such as Major General Aharon Yariv on the radio, using his wiles against a terrorist such as Captain Rifa'at in a private mental chess match, are gone forever. ■

Major General Aharon Yariv

PLANNING THE RESCUE

Operationally, Barak had one pressing requirement—to immobilize the aircraft so that the terrorists could not take the hostages out of Israel. He dispatched his best intelligence gatherers to get close to the aircraft. Under cover of darkness, they planted listening devices and also began to drain the plane's hydraulic fluids. Barak then focused on the real challenge—to find a solution to the hijacking before Captain Rifa'at's deadline was reached.

As Yariv and his staff kept a dialogue going with Captain Rifa'at, the Sayeret Mat'kal strike force prepared to assault the Sabena jetliner. Working inside a hangar at the other end of the airport, the commandos used a Boeing 707 just like the hijacked aircraft as a practice tool. The plan called for ladders to be hidden near the beseiged aircraft. Operators would use them to reach the wing and enter the plane.

The operators practiced the assault through the night and into the dawn of May 9. Surprise, Barak realized, would be the determining factor. If the commandos could get near the aircraft without attracting suspicion, then assaulting the jet would be no different from assaulting a building. Barak came up with an audacious plan.

Israeli authorities would behave as if they were surrendering to Captain Rifa'at's demands to release the 317 Palestinian prisoners. Meanwhile, the IDF would locate 317 Israeli soldiers who could pass as Palestinians. Wearing prison clothing, the soldiers would be taken to the tarmac within view of the Sabena cockpit. The Israeli thinking was the hijackers would feel like celebrating once they saw that they had forced the State of Israel to negotiate with terrorists. Thus they wouldn't object to having airport mechanics get the aircraft ready for its flight out of Israel. The plan was that the commandos, dressed as the mechanics, would use that moment to strike.

Operators of Sayeret Mat'kal wear the white overalls that disguised them as airport mechanics. IDF chief of staff Lieutenant General David Elazar is in the foreground.

THE RESCUE

Captain Rifa'at welcomed the news of Israel's decision to free the Palestinian prisoners with relief and pride. He then agreed that Israeli aircraft mechanics could fuel up the aircraft and ready it for flight. This was the cue the Mat'kal commandos were waiting for.

■ ■

Barak and his commandos, *wearing the same white coveralls that all aircraft mechanics at the airport wore, walked toward the besieged aircraft. The fake mechanics didn't appear threatening, nor were they carrying heavy firepower. Their semiautomatic pistols were nestled inside their coveralls. As the men neared the plane, they removed the ladders that had been hidden around the aircraft during the night.*

Barak gave his operators the signal to go. They hoisted the ladders to the wing and, just as they had perfected in training, positioned themselves near the main door. They removed their pistols and cocked them to ensure there was one round in the chamber. Sweating under the hot May sun, Barak ordered his men inside the aircraft.

The flood of men in white coveralls flowing through the narrow aisle of the Boeing 707 took the hijackers—and the hostages— completely by surprise. The assault was so dynamic, so swift, and so unexpected that the terrorist response was instinctive. Instead of detonating their explosive devices and destroying the plane, the terrorists grabbed their sidearms and attempted to resist. One commando cut down the male terrorist named Abdel Aziz al-Atrash with a burst of gunfire. One of the female terrorists, Ruma Isa Tarus, was on the floor,

Lieutenant Colonel Ehud Barak (left) oversees the release of hostages from the hijacked Sabena Airlines plane.

clutching a grenade with its safety pin removed. Another commando grabbed the grenade from her and put the pin back in to disarm it. He pushed her, unharmed, toward the support personnel who were leading the hostages off the aircraft. Standing near the cockpit, Captain Rifa'at was firing his pistol wildly and was killed in a burst of fire from one of the Mat'kal operators. The last terrorist, Tirza Halsah, was wounded.

The raid, which would become known as Operation Isotope 1, took ninety seconds to execute. Both male Palestinian terrorists were killed. Both female terrorists were captured and later sentenced to lengthy prison terms. One hostage, a young woman who leaped to her feet the moment the commandos announced their entry, was killed by an exchange of gunfire.

■ ■

Operation Isotope 1 showed that select groups of specially trained operators could succeed against gun-wielding terrorists. The terrorism and counterterrorism chess match was forever altered.

The dramatic Sabena hijacking and rescue drew a lot of media attention. But the events of September 1972 made the world aware of the full extent of Palestinian terrorism. During the Summer Olympic Games that month in Munich, West Germany, members of Black September took hostage eleven members of the Israeli Olympic team. The world watched as the drama was played out to a horrific end. The West German government would not allow Sayeret Mat'kal to attempt a rescue. A failed rescue attempt by West German police ended with the terrorists killing all the athletes.

The global community witnessed the horrific drama of the Black September attack on Israeli athletes in 1972 at the Munich Olympic Games. A masked terrorist *(top)* on a balcony became the symbol of the Munich Olympic Massacre.

The Munich Olympic Massacre changed the way nations—particularly Israel—fought terrorism. The Israeli government dedicated its military and intelligence services to finding the Palestinians responsible for the attack. It also set up a counterterrorist unit called Ya'ma'm to cover hostage rescues within Israel. But Sayeret Mat'kal was still tasked with hostage rescues beyond Israel's borders. The unit again got the call when hijackers seized an Air France flight.

OPERATION THUNDERBALL, ENTEBBE, UGANDA, JULY 3–4, 1976 | Terrorists are constantly devising attack

schemes that will thwart rescue attempts by police and military counterterrorist units. If hostages could be held far from a nation's frontiers, the nation's counterterrorist forces might not be able to attempt a rescue. Then the operation would be an unbridled success.

Wadi Haddad, the master planner of the Popular Front for the Liberation of Palestine (PFLP), had scoured the world for just such an approach to a hijacking operation. His carefully mapped hijacking would involve Germany's Red Army Faction (RAF), whose goal of global revolution put it in league with Palestinian terrorists like the PFLP. Haddad's plan would eventually bring the hostages to Uganda in East Africa, far from the clutches of Israel's commandos.

THE HIJACKING

On the morning of June 27, 1976, four passengers—two Germans of the RAF and two Palestinians of the PFLP—disembarked from Singapore Airlines Flight 763 at Athens International Airport in Greece. They headed toward the gate for Air France Flight 139, which had originated in Tel Aviv, Israel. After the brief stopover in the Greek capital, Flight 139 would continue toward Paris. The weather was good, and the aircraft's captain, Michel Bacos, expected to bring his jet to Paris on schedule.

Security at Athens International Airport was typically weak. Nobody was on duty at the metal detector in the passenger corridor, and the police officer screening the luggage wasn't paying much attention to his monitor. The lax security allowed the four armed passengers from the Singapore Airlines flight to board the French aircraft with ease.

At 12:20 P.M., when the plane was at an altitude of 31,000 feet, the four passengers made their move. The German woman, Gabriele

Tiedemann, raced toward the first-class cabin with a gun and grenade in her hand. Meanwhile, farther up the aisle, the other German, Wilfred Böse, and the two Palestinian accomplices burst through the cockpit doors and announced that the aircraft had been hijacked in the name of Palestine. They ordered the captain to head to Libya in North Africa and then on to Uganda in East Africa.

News of the hijacking soon reached Paris and Tel Aviv. The Israeli government monitored the progress of Flight 139 toward Libya, a country friendly to terrorists. Some Israeli officials believed that this hijacking would be a French matter, because France owned the aircraft. But the hostages included many Jews and Israeli citizens. As a result, many inside Israel's intelligence and special operations communities suspected that their services would eventually be required to end the passengers' ordeal.

Later that afternoon, Flight 139 landed in Benghazi, Libya, where two more PFLP operatives boarded and the plane was refueled. At just after midnight on June 28, 1976, Air France Flight 139 touched down in Entebbe, Uganda, an airfield near the capital city of Kampala.

Ugandan soldiers and AK47-toting PFLP operatives immediately surrounded the plane. Ugandan president Idi Amin Dada, who had once been trained by Israeli paratroopers, had turned away from Israel. He now promoted the causes of

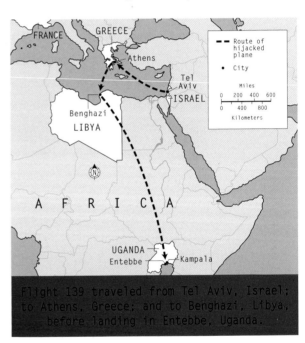

Flight 139 traveled from Tel Aviv, Israel; to Athens, Greece; and to Benghazi, Libya, before landing in Entebbe, Uganda.

Palestinian liberation groups, including the destruction of Israel.

Ugandan soldiers guarded the hostages and surrounded the airport. During the next forty-eight hours, the PFLP took responsibility for the hijacking and demanded the release of Palestinian prisoners in European and Israeli jails. If all the listed prisoners were not released by July 1, the terrorists would blow up the plane and the hostages.

The terrorists also separated Jews and Israelis from the other hostages, releasing those without a connection to the State of Israel. The

Israeli government couldn't sit idly by as Germans and Palestinians slaughtered its citizens. And no solutions were coming from the French government. The Israelis ordered the IDF to prepare a rescue plan. As expected, the situation had become an Israeli matter.

FIRST STEPS

Sayeret Mat'kal, commanded by Lieutenant Colonel Yonatan "Yoni"

Lieutenant Colonel
Yoni Netanyahu

Netanyahu, was tasked with the rescue. But Mat'kal was too small to successfully occupy an airfield for an hour. For this job, the IDF summoned paratroopers, infantry, and the air force. It was also clear the IDF operation would have to use huge Hercules C-130s, aircraft that could reach Uganda from Israel without refueling.

The non-Jewish hostages were flown back to Paris, where Israeli intelligence agents debriefed each one. The released hostages revealed how many Palestinian and German guards were at the terminal and how many Ugandan soldiers surrounded the airport. The released hostages told the agents that they'd been held in Entebbe's Old Terminal. (This building, though no longer used, had been built by an Israeli construction company, which supplied the layout.) Flights were still landing at the New Terminal.

Any raid so far from home base requires extra stealth and surprise. Stealth was assured because the Israeli C-130s were going to make their approach close behind an inbound British passenger jet. It was hoped that radar operators at the main airfield would not be able to distinguish the passenger plane from the other aircraft flying closely behind.

Surprise on the ground was harder. Ugandan soldiers surrounded the Old Terminal. Sayeret Mat'kal officers realized that any trick that bought even a few seconds was valuable. They needed a cushion from the moment when the Israeli C-130s landed to the time when the vehicles and soldiers reached the terminal. These seconds could be the difference between life and death for the Mat'kal operators and the hostages. With this in mind, an ingenious—if farfetched—plan was conceived.

THE ALMIGHTY HERCULES

The one aircraft that has earned the complete trust of special operations units around the world is the Hercules C-130. Capable of taking off and landing in rough fields, the aircraft is the primary transport used by more than sixty nations. Known affectionately as the Herc, the aircraft was immortalized in the Entebbe rescue.

AIRCRAFT SPECIFICATIONS

Power Plant: Four Allison T56-A-15 turboprops; 4,300 horsepower, each engine

Length: 97 feet 9 inches

Height: 38 feet 3 inches

Wingspan: 132 feet 7 inches

Speed: 374 mph at 20,000 feet

Range: 2,356 miles with maximum payload; 2,500 miles with 25,000 pounds cargo; 5,200 miles with no cargo.

Crew: Five (two pilots, a navigator, a flight engineer, and a loadmaster)

Maximum Takeoff Weight: 155,000 pounds

Maximum Usable Fuel: 60,000 pounds

Maximum Allowable Cabin Load: 36,000 pounds

Normal Passenger Seats Available: Up to 92 troops or 64 paratroops or 74 patients on litters ■

The hard-working Herc

PLANNING THE RESCUE

The plan required the lead force of Mat'kal commandos to masquerade as President Amin's motorcade. The thinking was that no Ugandan soldier in his right mind would dare to stop the black Mercedes sedan carrying their national leader. Other members of the lead force of Mat'kal commandos would be disguised as Amin's security service.

While the planning was going on, Prime Minister Yitzhak Rabin helped secure landing rights in Kenya, Israel's sole political ally in East Africa. The C-130s would then be able to refuel in Nairobi, Kenya's capital, before the return flight to Israel. Meanwhile, Rabin called in Idi Amin's old IDF paratroop commander to delay the hostage deadline by holding out the possibility of ending the crisis through negotiations.

The ploy worked, and the PFLP announced that Israel and the European nations had until 2:00 P.M. on July 4, 1976, to release the prisoners. Because of the lengthy flight to Entebbe, Rabin ordered the commandos to take off from Israel and await authorization while in the air. At 1:20 P.M., the five C-130s (four transports and a converted hospital aircraft) lifted off. The cabinet reached its decision unanimously: it was a go. The operation was code-named Thunderball, after a James Bond film.

THE RESCUE

The seven-hour journey to Entebbe was long and hard. The C-130s skirted Egyptian and Saudi radar by flying low and bounced through some of the worst thunderstorms ever recorded over East Africa. Miraculously, at 11:01 P.M., only thirty seconds behind schedule, the pilot of the lead Hercules touched down at Entebbe.

■ ■

The vehicles designed to imitate Amin's motorcade were on the ground and moving away before the Hercules rolled to a stop. They moved down the connecting road to the Old Terminal as fast as they could. Some fifty yards from the terminal, the motorcade encountered a Ugandan checkpoint whose soldiers weren't fooled by the Israelis' disguises. While they had suspected the masquerade, they were too slow to deal with the invasion. Mat'kal commandos blew the guards away in a flurry of fire.

The Mat'kal commandos ran the last forty yards to the Old

Mat'kal commandos load up the black Mercedes sedan that was used to imitate Ugandan president Idi Amin Dada's motorcade.

Terminal on foot. As they raced into the building, Ugandan soldiers began firing their weapons. But the Mat'kal sharpshooters neutralized each source of fire with quick bursts of fire.

The German and Palestinian terrorists opened fire on the hostages, who were asleep on cots and on the floor. The Mat'kal operators had to identify and eliminate the sources of terrorist gunfire and also calm down the hostages.

Gabriele Tiedemann was hit by a burst from an operator's Uzi submachine gun. Wilfred Böse was cut in two by a five-round burst from an AK-47. Commandos carrying bullhorns shouted "We are the IDF! Stay Down!" in English and in Hebrew, but several of the hostages stood to applaud the rescue. Three were killed in the exchange.

The Mat'kal commandos were busy gathering the hostages for the mad dash to the tarmac, where the C-130s awaited them. The commandos urged the hostages to move quickly because the airport had erupted into a pitched battle. In fact, during the chaos, Lieutenant Colonel Netanyahu was killed by a round of bullets.

The rescue took all of three minutes. With the hostages secure, the other ground units began the most important element of the operation—destroying the Ugandan air force. The Israelis feared that the Ugandan air force would attempt to shoot down the slow-moving Hercules transports.

With clockwork precision, armored personnel carriers roared off the ramp of the second C-130 transport to take up positions at the front and rear of the Old Terminal. Infantry from the first and third planes ran to secure all access to roads to the airport. Firing antitank rockets, Israeli forces destroyed Uganda's Soviet-made MiG17 fighters. The aircraft, parked neatly in several rows of four, went up in a fireball of jet fuel and intense heat. With the airfield secure, the hostages were ushered onto the fourth Hercules for the flight back to Israel.

■ ■

The entire ground operation at Entebbe took fifty-eight minutes. Twenty Ugandan soldiers were killed in the operation, and all six terrorists were dead. After a brief stopover in Nairobi, Kenya, for fuel, the aerial armada headed home to Israel.

When the first Hercules C-130 touched down, hundreds of soldiers, officials, and relatives greeted the hostages. Special attention was give to Captain Michel Bacos and his crew, who had refused to leave the Jewish and Israeli hostages, even though the terrorists had offered to release the crew.

The raid on Entebbe was a remarkable expression of one nation's refusal to succumb to extortion and murder, but it had come with a price. One of the C-130s unloaded the Mat'kal commandos who had made the rescue possible. Somber and exhausted, the commandos neither rejoiced nor felt relief. Instead, they felt anguish and loss as they carried out the body of their slain commander.

Hostages emerge to a joyous welcome at Ben Gurion International Airport in Israel. Captain Michel Bacos, skipper of the hijacked plane, is at far left.

WHO'S WHO AND
WHAT'S WHAT

Foreign Legion: founded in 1831, a volunteer fighting unit of the French government

French Empire: the historic holdings of the nation of France, including its colonies and territories in Africa, Asia, the Caribbean, and South America. Algeria in North Africa was part of this empire, until a bitter nationalist revolt from 1954 to 1961 won the country its independence in 1962. The French Territory of the Afars and Issas, another imperial holding, won independence in 1977.

French Territory of the Afars and Issas: from 1967 to 1977, the name of a colony of France in East Africa. It was called French Somaliland from 1885 to 1967. After 1977, the region became the independent nation of Djibouti. The Afars and the Issas are the two major ethnic groups in Djibouti.

Front for the Liberation of the Coast of Somalia (FLCS): a terrorist group whose goal was to gain independence for the French Territory of the Afars and Issas and to make French forces leave the area

Groupe d'Intervention de la Gendarmerie Nationale (GIGN): formed in 1974, France's premier counterterrorist and hostage-rescue force

Groupe Islamique Armé (GIA): formed in 1992, a terrorist group whose goal is to establish an Islamic government in Algeria

TERRORIST DOSSIERS

Islamic fundamentalism: a school of thought that supports the return to traditional Islamic ideas and government. Most Islamic fundamentalists do not advocate terrorism.

Lieutenant Christian Prouteau: the founder of GIGN and its first commander

Major Denis Favier: the commander of GIGN during the 1994 Marseilles rescue

Somalia: an independent nation in East Africa that resulted from the 1960 union of the colonies of British Somaliland and Italian Somaliland

special weapons and tactics (SWAT): a term referring to the special police units trained to use military weapons and maneuvers

RESCUES BY FRANCE'S GIGN

The 1972 Munich Olympic Massacre was a horrific wake-up call to European security officials, including those in France. Many French officials feared that it would only be a matter of time before France faced a Munich of its own. That wake-up call came in 1973, when Palestinian terrorists took over the Saudi Arabian embassy in Paris. Although the hostages were eventually released, the French government realized it needed its own counterterrorist and hostage-rescue force. The Groupe d'Intervention de la Gendarmerie Nationale (GIGN, or Intervention Group of the National Police) was created on March 10, 1974, as part of the French national police force.

DEADLINE IN FRENCH TERRITORY, FEBRUARY 3–4, 1976 | The GIGN's first operation happened in East Africa, far from France. The first assignment was to rescue children held captive by an obscure and extremely violent national liberation movement in the French Territory of the Afars and Issas.

THE HIJACKING

On the morning of February 3, 1976, four terrorists from the Front for the Liberation of the Coast of Somalia (FLCS) hijacked a school bus carrying thirty students. They were the children of French air force personnel stationed in the French Territory of the Afars and Issas.

The FLCS terrorists forced the bus driver to drive southward to the border with Somalia, a neighboring independent nation that was supportive of the French Territory's drive for self-rule. At a prearranged spot, a fifth hijacker boarded the bus. The terrorists had hoped to take the bus into Somalia, but the Foreign Legion—a fighting unit of the French government stationed in French colonies—had successfully stopped the bus six hundred feet from the Somalian frontier. A standoff ensued. The Legionnaires surrounded the bus, while Somalian border police, in support of the terrorists, aimed their weapons at the troops.

The Legionnaires were not trained in the delicate art of hostage rescue. Adding to the local commander's concern was the terrorists' demand. Unless France granted immediate independence to the French Territory, they would begin executing the children one by one. The commander realized this was an assignment that only the GIGN could take on. The Legionnaires secured the area around the bus and waited for the arrival of a unit that had never before been tested in a true counterterrorist setting.

The GIGN's first assignment was in a faraway part of the old French Empire in Africa.

FIRST STEPS

The GIGN commander, Lieutenant Christian Prouteau, flew to the territory with his task force. He was facing a difficult scenario. The five terrorists were armed with AK-47 assault rifles. They were receiving tacit support from Somalian soldiers across the barren frontier. The hostages were all children, a reality that even seasoned counterterrorist operators found emotionally draining.

Lieutenant Prouteau understood the operational challenge, and he realized that the response had to be unique and decisive. His plan required absolute surprise, surprise that could only be achieved through the skills of top-notch snipers.

PLANNING THE RESCUE

Prouteau decided he would have his marksmen pick off the five terrorists simultaneously to take away the threat to the children. But what if one of the kids suddenly jumped up during the precision assault? Prouteau realized he would have to remove the children from the equation altogether. When the terrorists agreed to allow food to be brought on the bus, GIGN operators had the sandwiches doped with mild tranquilizers. The tranquilizers needed at least a half hour to take effect.

The rescue plan called for the snipers to hit each terrorist with one shot to the head. The moment the snipers fired their weapons, the GIGN task force would then board the bus and remove the children from harm's way. The Legionnaires, itching to get involved, were tasked with keeping the terrorists' Somalian accomplices busy with a wall of machine gun and mortar fire.

THE RESCUE

An hour after the children ate their sandwiches, Lieutenant Prouteau noticed the children slumbering in their seats. Everything was up to the snipers.

SNIPER

In the world of special operations, snipers are a unique breed. They can be detached and moody. They are trained to operate alone. Snipers take it upon themselves to kill at a distance, preferably with one shot, and then to disappear.

Snipers must be able to move silently and anonymously through hostile terrain. They must be willing to lay in wait, often in the harshest weather, until they get that split-second opportunity to use their precision weapons. ∎

A GIGN sniper suited up for action

■ ■

At 3:57 P.M., Prouteau gave the order to fire. The snipers, trained to hit a dime from five hundred yards away, had compensated for the range, the sun, the wind, and the angles of the bullets hitting the glass windows. All hit their targets in their heads. The children, knocked out by the tranquilizers, didn't panic, but they still had to be rescued.

The GIGN assault force raced toward the bus. Foreign Legion mortar and machine guns peppered Somalian lines with a barrage of dedicated fire. But one of the soldiers had crossed over from Somalia and had managed to get near the bus. Before the GIGN team could evacuate the children, he fired his weapon into the bus, killing a five-year-old girl. The soldier was immediately killed by a burst of GIGN machine-gun fire.

■ ■

Despite the painful loss of one hostage, the GIGN had brilliantly executed its first hostage-rescue operation. In the ensuing years, the GIGN would gain valuable experience as both a military special operations unit and as a SWAT force. There would be more hostage rescues and counterterrorist work in the mountains between France and Spain. The GIGN would also take on assignments in other parts of the old French Empire, including Algeria in North Africa.

ASSAULT ON AIR FRANCE FLIGHT 8969, DECEMBER 24–27, 1994

In the early 1990s, a growing and violent Islamic fundamentalist movement in Algeria had spawned the Groupe Islamique Armé (GIA, or Armed Islamic Group), one of the world's most brutal terrorist groups. By 1994 the French government had dispatched the GIGN to assist in security operations at the French embassy in Algiers, the capital of Algeria.

THE HIJACKING

At 11:00 A.M. on December 24, 1994, Air France Flight 8969 was at its gate, getting ready to taxi for takeoff from Algiers International Airport. The flight crew had just completed its mandatory safety presentation, and the pilot spoke of the routine nature of the two-hour flight to Orly International Airport in Paris.

In addition to the 12 members of the crew, 227 passengers were on board. Many of them were French women and children who were fleeing massacre-plagued Algeria at the behest of French husbands and fathers still working in the former French colony.

Yet before the aircraft could pull away from the gate, four young men wearing airport coveralls boarded the aircraft. They told the bewildered flight crew that they were security officials and proceeded to check the passports of the passengers. But the men suddenly closed the cabin's doors, produced assault pistols, and told the stunned passengers that the GIA was hijacking the plane.

FIRST STEPS

News of the Air France hijacking reached Paris within the hour. The French government told Major Denis Favier, commander of the GIGN, to get his unit ready. Another Air France plane flew the team to Palma de Mallorca in Spain, a short chopper ride from Algiers. If the terrorists started killing the hostages, the GIGN would have to deploy immediately. Initially, however, news from the hijacked aircraft showed signs that the terrorists wanted to resolve the ordeal peacefully. The hijackers released women and children and entered into a dialogue with Algerian authorities.

Major Denis Favier

PLANNING THE RESCUE

The GIA terrorists issued their demands on the morning of Christmas Day. Unless two imprisoned terrorist leaders were released, all the hostages would be killed and the aircraft destroyed. As the negotiators talked and as the hostages suffered in fear, the hijackers snapped. At just after noon on Christmas Day, the terrorists killed a hostage who worked for the French embassy and dumped his body on the tarmac. The man had been shot in the back of the head. For the French government, the cold-blooded killing of a French embassy employee was a signal that the terrorists would not listen to reason. The hijacking had to end immediately.

The GIGN was given a green light to take down the aircraft, and the unit prepared to fly from Spain to Algiers. But fearing the political ramifications of having French soldiers once again operating on Algerian soil, the Algerian government gave the hijacked plane permission to take off and to choose its destination. Fatefully, the hijackers chose Marseilles, France. The French government authorized the GIGN to move in.

Major Favier's assault force consisted of forty operators. Snipers were ready to fire when given the OK. Other operators masqueraded as airport workers to get closer to the aircraft. They planted microphones and high-tech monitoring devices to track the terrorists throughout the aircraft.

Flight 8969 on the ground in Algiers, Christmas Day, 1994

THE RESCUE

■ ■

Fifty-four hours into the crisis, the GIGN made its move. Pulling down black masks, the assault force split into two parts and approached the plane from the tail section. Twenty-five operators positioned themselves on the tarmac underneath the aircraft. Fifteen slowly began climbing a mobile staircase that had been left near the front right door.

Feeling that a French attack was soon to come, the four hijackers had entered the cockpit. One of the terrorists opened the cockpit window and began firing his AK-47 at the control tower. The lead GIGN operator, on the stairs and poised to enter the aircraft, threw a stun grenade (an explosive device) squarely through the open pane of glass. A bright orange glow, followed by a thud, indicated that the device had detonated properly. It was time to storm the aircraft.

The lead assault team went in through a hail of AK-47 fire. As part of the GIGN force engaged the terrorists in the cockpit, the rest of the assault force quickly secured the cabin to make sure no other terrorists were hiding with the hostages.

The GIGN operators yelled in French that they were the French police, as they ushered everyone off on the aircraft's orange emergency chutes. Fifty ambulances rushed the hostages to safety. Nearly a dozen had been wounded by stray bullets and by the stampede toward the emergency exits.

Securing the aircraft took all of ninety seconds. Only the cockpit was unsecured. The four terrorists had no place to go. GIGN snipers in the control tower, monitoring the silhouettes through their rifle scopes, killed the terrorists inside of a minute. At 5:35 P.M., Major Favier sent a message to the control tower signaling the end of the ordeal.

A team of GIGN operators assaults the hijacked Air France plane after it had landed near Marseilles, France.

The Christmas Miracle in Marseilles, as many in the French media proclaimed it, took all of twenty minutes—from the rolling of the mobile stairs to the identification of the hostages on the tarmac. Twenty-five

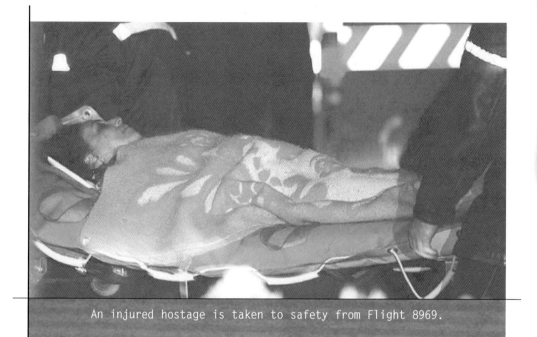

An injured hostage is taken to safety from Flight 8969.

people were injured in the assault, including several GIGN operators. All of the terrorists were killed. On December 27, 1994, the hostages, as well as the GIGN operators, arrived at Orly Airport in Paris to tumultuous applause. President François Mitterrand personally congratulated each member of the GIGN rescue force.

WHO'S WHO AND WHAT'S WHAT

Bijzondere Bijstands Eenheid (BBE): the main counterterrorist unit of the Netherlands

Captain Jurgen Schumann: the original pilot of the Lufthansa Flight 181. During the hijacking, Captain Mahmoud, the leader of the Palestinian hijackers, executed him.

Captain Mahmoud: the false name of international terrorist Zohair Youssef Akache, who led the hijacking of Lufthansa Flight 181. He was killed during the rescue operation.

Colonel Ulrich Wegener: the founder and first commander of Germany's GSG-9 counterterrorist force

F-104 Starfighter: a single-seat turbojet fighter built by the U.S. Air Force but used by many other nations, including the Netherlands

Grenzschutzgruppe 9 (GSG-9): Germany's main counterterrorist unit

Royal Netherlands Marine Corps: the military group from which the BBE draws its members

South Moluccas: a small group of islands that have been incorporated into far southeastern Indonesia since the 1950s. The people of the South Moluccas continue to seek independence.

RESCUES BY THE DUTCH BBE AND GERMANY'S GSG-9

By the mid-1970s, after the horror of the Munich Olympic Massacre, European nations had slowly come to terms with the realities of large-scale terrorism. The Netherlands created the Bijzondere Bijstands Eenheid (BBE, or Close Combat Unit) soon after Munich as part of the Royal Netherlands Marine Corps. Germany's Grenzschutzgruppe 9 (GSG-9, or Border Protection Group 9) was established as a direct result of West Germany's inept response to the terrorist attack at the Olympic Games. By 1977 both forces were fully operational, and both carried out spectacular hostage rescues that year.

BBE's RESCUE AT DE PUNT, MAY 23–JUNE 11, 1977

At one time, the Netherlands had colonies throughout the world. The Dutch East Indies—the modern-day archipelago of Indonesia—brought the small European country vast wealth. One of the archipelago's ethnic minority groups was the South Moluccans of southeastern Indonesia.

From 1945 to 1949, during the fight for Indonesian independence, the South Moluccans fought alongside the Dutch in the hope of later gaining self-rule. But the Dutch lost the war, and many of the South Moluccan volunteers moved to the Netherlands, where they were promised better lives. Instead, many were thrust into abject poverty and discrimination.

By the early 1970s, the second-generation of South Moluccans in the Netherlands had become angry at the bitter lives their families were forced to lead. Inspired by the stories of Palestinian terrorists, some South Moluccans created their own terrorist underground that sought independence for their homeland through violence.

THE HIJACKING

On the morning of May 23, 1977, nine young South Moluccan men, all heavily armed with submachine guns and grenades, seized control of a passenger train at De Punt, the Netherlands, with 94 people on board. Simultaneously, four other South Moluccan terrorists took over a schoolhouse at the Dutch town of Bovensmilde that held 105 children and 4 teachers.

The hijacked train sits on the tracks at De Punt, the Netherlands, in 1977. Food was brought in to the hostages during the ordeal.

The Dutch government entered into negotiations with the terrorists that dragged on for three weeks. Finally, on June 11, the Dutch government ordered the BBE to end the ordeals in both locations.

THE RESCUE

■ ■

At Bovensmilde on June 11, the BBE was deployed behind a protective shield of the Royal Netherlands Military Police. The operators positioned themselves outside the school, and when the order was given, their entry was fast and decisive. The terrorists were overwhelmed by the massive show of force as the BBE operators, clutching their machine guns, flooded the location. The schoolhouse was liberated without bloodshed, with all hostages rescued.

■ ■

The train at De Punt was a different story. Any hope of a peaceful outcome was lost when the hijackers killed the train engineer and threw his body off the train. Intelligence on what was going on inside the isolated train was hard to come by. The terrorists were wary of potential government attempts to mount an assault. In fact, they insisted that all food deliveries be made by police officers who were stripped naked to ensure they were not armed.

PLANNING THE RESCUE

Using identical railway cars, the BBE set up a duplicate version of the train. The operators spent the three weeks of the standoff honing their skills for the one chance they would get at assaulting the real train.

At De Punt, the BBE came up with a unique diversion to give them a few precious extra seconds as they struggled with access points to the train. Seconds before the assault was to start, two Royal Netherlands Air Force F-104 Starfighters would make a low-level pass over the train. It was hoped that the resulting sonic boom would be so powerful that it would shock the gunmen who were poised to repel any rescue attempt.

BBE operators train to carry out a lightning-fast assault on the train.

THE RESCUE

■ ■

On June 11, just before the two F-104 Starfighters made their pass over the besieged train, BBE operators placed explosive charges at the front of the train. Two teams of BBE operators, one assault force and the other providing cover fire, moved slowly and silently through a high field of grass toward the train as the planes neared. When the afterburners and the bombs blasted through the early morning air, the assault commenced. The diversion and assault plans worked brilliantly.

The BBE's entrance into the train was executed with great speed. Within seconds, doors and windows had been breached, and six of the nine terrorists had been killed. Three others were captured. Tragically, two hostages were also killed.

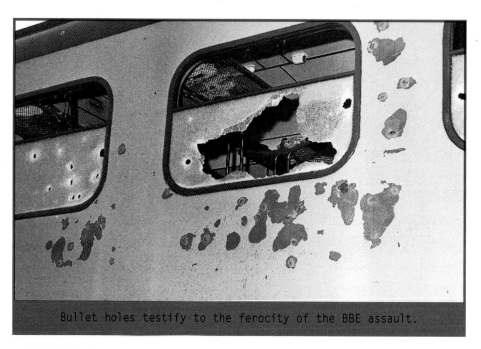

Bullet holes testify to the ferocity of the BBE assault.

■ ■

The rescue had taken two minutes. For virtually every counterterrorist force in the world seriously dedicated to rescuing hostages, the BBE's assault at De Punt remains a textbook lesson plan.

OPERATION MAGIC FIRE, MOGADISHU, SOMALIA, OCTOBER 13–17, 1977 | The operators of

GSG-9, West Germany's first true counterterrorist unit, embody the resolve of their nation (modern unified Germany) to prevent another Munich Olympic Massacre from happening. The unit showed this commitment to the world in 1977, when Palestinian terrorists hijacked a German plane and demanded that the West German government free prisoners from the RAF, West Germany's home-grown terrorist group.

THE HIJACKING

On October 13, 1977, just after 1:00 P.M., Lufthansa Flight 181—filled with German vacationers returning home after a holiday in Spain—lifted off from Palma de Mallorca International Airport. One hour into the journey, the plane's skipper, Captain Jurgen Schumann, radioed air traffic control that the aircraft had been hijacked and that he had been ordered to fly to Rome, Italy.

Shortly after Schumann's initial broadcast, a man who identified himself only as Captain Mahmoud reaffirmed that the plane had been hijacked. (It would later come to light that Mahmoud was loosely associated with the RAF and the PFLP.)

He was demanding that Germany release virtually all RAF terrorists in its prisons, as well as provide the hijackers with roughly $20 million in ransom. If the demands were not met, Captain Mahmoud said, the hostages would be summarily shot and the plane destroyed.

First Steps

The moment Flight 181 was hijacked, an alarm was sounded at the headquarters of the GSG-9. Its founder and commanding officer, Colonel Ulrich Wegener, had witnessed the debacle at Munich and had vowed that Germany would never again be held hostage to terrorists. Wegener prepared GSG-9 to deploy to Rome.

Planning the Rescue

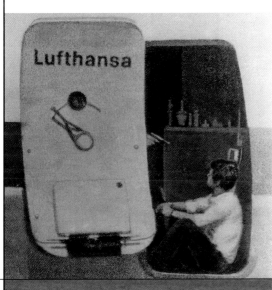

Captain Jurgen Schumann sits in the doorway of Flight 181, facing the gun of Captain Mahmoud. The hijacker would later execute Schumann.

In Rome, Flight 181 was refueled and readied for immediate takeoff. While the plane was on the ground, Captain Schumann had managed to open his cabin window and drop four cigarette boxes outside, a hint to authorities that there were four terrorists on the aircraft. GSG-9 was awaiting government approval to fly to Rome, when the aircraft suddenly radioed the ground control tower that it was taking off. For the next seventy-two hours, Flight 181 crisscrossed the Mediterranean and the Middle East.

Captain Mahmoud proved to be a cold-blooded hijacker during this initial phase of the operation. Suspecting that Captain Schumann had secretly communicated with the German government, Captain Mahmoud summarily shot him through the back of his head. For the remainder of the ordeal, the copilot Jurgen Vietor flew Flight 181. Eventually, it ended up in East Africa, in the Somalian capital of Mogadishu, with GSG-9 simply following its flight path.

Colonel Ulrich Wegener accepts a medal for his work during Operation Magic Fire.

The West Germans received the full support and cooperation of the Somalian authorities at Mogadishu Airport. A West German official was flown to Somalia to talk to Captain Mahmoud on the radio. He assured the hijacker that as long as he extended the deadline for killing the hostages, the West German government would release eleven of the RAF terrorists. It was a clever ruse. Colonel Wegener guessed that Captain Mahmoud, once confident that he had won, would be less wary of an attack than if negotiations were at a standstill and the deadline was looming.

Wegener's plan had two separate diversions. In the first, Somalian soldiers would set off a large bonfire in front of the cockpit. With Captain Mahmoud preoccupied by the light erupting across the tarmac, GSG-9 would strike with stun grenades, the second diversion. Once the stun grenades were inside the aircraft, the GSG-9 entry team would have an edge to kill the terrorists before they could kill the hostages.

THE RESCUE

■ ■

As planned, the GSG-9 operators used the diversion of the Somalian fire to climb the wings of the Boeing 737 undetected. Snipers positioned throughout the airfield monitored the operators' movement. The attack force entered the aircraft through the emergency doors. The lead operators hurled their stun grenades down the aisles, before racing through the aircraft with their weapons cocked and ready.

Once inside the aircraft, the GSG-9 operators shouted to the hostages to keep down. Captain Mahmoud was found first. He was killed by a well-placed burst of MP5 submachine-gun fire. As he charged down the aisle, an operator killed one of the female terrorists with a 9mm burst to the head. Submachine-gun fire fatally wounded a third terrorist. The fourth terrorist, a Palestinian female, was critically injured during the assault and was apprehended.

■ ■

STUN GRENADE

Many special operations missions start with the pulling of a pin and the tossing of a grenade that is designed to do nothing more than explode in a blinding flash and a deafening roar. The diversionary device, called a flash-bang, has become an invaluable tool in virtually any type of tactical operations—from high-risk arrests to hostage-rescue raids. Some stun grenades, once launched, are designed to race uncontrollably around a room, like a pinball in a machine. Others simply create a few seconds of disorientation.

This exploding device usually causes terrorists to cower, while they cover their eyes and ears. Meanwhile, counterterrorist and hostage-rescue forces seize the initiative. Stun grenades apply the least amount of force necessary to gain precious seconds of surprise. ■

Less than five minutes after the first GSG-9 operator stormed into the Boeing 737, the ordeal was over. Colonel Wegener sent a message to Bonn, the capital of West Germany over a secure radio frequency that the terrorists had been eliminated and the hostages freed.

By dawn's first light, planes carried the hostages back to West Germany. The GSG-9 operators were also in the air, heading home for a hero's welcome.

Captain E.: the leader of the NOCS team that rescued General Dozier. The captain's full name is still classified.

Communism: a social and political theory based on the idea that property and industry should be owned by the whole community rather than by individuals

Democratic Front for the Liberation of Arabistan (DFLA): a little-known terrorist group whose goal was to win independence for Arabistan, the old name for the province of Khuzestan in southwestern Iran. The group objected to the policies of the new Iranian regime of the Ayatollah Ruhollah Khomeini established in 1979.

James Dozier: U.S. Army brigadier general. At the time of his kidnapping, Dozier was the highest-ranking North Atlantic Treaty Organization (NATO) commander in Italy.

North Atlantic Treaty Organization (NATO): a defensive alliance established in 1949 between the United States and European nations. Its Southern Command includes Italy.

Nucleo Operativo Centrale di Sicurezza (NOCS): formed in 1978, the counterterrorist commando unit of Italy's state police force

Oan: the leader of the six terrorists who took over the Iranian embassy

rappel: a method of descending vertical heights, such as high walls, by dropping down a rope

Red Brigades: a terrorist group most active in Italy in the 1970s and 1980s. It wanted to overthrow Italy's government and replace it with a Communist system.

Scotland Yard: the headquarters of the London Metropolitan Police force. Its specialist operations (SO) units include an antiterrorist branch (SO13) and a diplomatic protection branch (SO16).

Special Air Service (SAS): Great Britain's military counterterrorist force

RESCUES BY
BRITAIN'S SAS
AND ITALY'S NOCS

Great Britain's Special Air Service (SAS) dates to World War II (1939–1945), when the British army sent highly trained troops deep behind enemy lines. SAS units gathered intelligence, organized sabotage, and carried out every kind of covert operation. By the 1970s, the SAS had become one of the best special operations forces in the world. But after the 1972 Munich Olympic Massacre, the SAS added counterterrorism and hostage rescue to its portfolio.

Similarly, Italy had long been battling internal criminals, such as the Mafia, but in the 1970s, it needed a unit specifically trained to combat terrorism and to protect foreign dignitaries. Italy's Nucleo Operativo Centrale di Sicurezza (NOCS, or Central Security Operation Unit) came into being in 1978 as part of the country's state police.

Both the SAS and NOCS would be busy in the 1980s. They would have success in high-profile hostage rescues played on a world stage.

The winged dagger, with its motto "Who Dares Wins," has been the SAS's insignia since World War II.

OPERATION NIMROD, LONDON, ENGLAND, APRIL 30–MAY 5, 1980 |
Over the years, the SAS had earned a reputation for fast deployment and efficiency under dire circumstances. These qualities came into play in a hostage rescue in London, the British capital.

THE HOSTAGE TAKING

At 11:30 A.M. on April 30, 1980, six members of the Democratic Front for the Liberation of Arabistan (DFLA), a little-known anti-Iranian terrorist group, burst into the Iranian embassy at 16 Princes Gate in London. The terrorists fired their weapons wildly as they stormed the structure and quickly seized control of the building. The more than twenty people inside the building, including a British police officer on a routine inspection, became hostages.

Few British officials had ever heard of the DFLA and its desire to gain independence for Arabistan, an oil-rich province in southwestern Iran. In addition, the terrorists' demands were completely unrealistic. If the world did not recognize the legitimate rights of the people of Arabistan and if the Iranian authorities did not release nearly one hundred Arabistani prisoners by May 1, 1980, the terrorists said they would kill all the hostages and blow up the embassy.

FIRST STEPS

Scotland Yard received word of the terrorist takeover of the embassy shortly after the first shots were fired. The police officer inside was a member of SO16, the London Metropolitan Police's elite diplomatic protection group. He activated an electronic beeper on his lapel that alerted police to the unfolding emergency. Within moments, police officers from SO13, the counterterrorism section, and from other branches rushed to the embassy and surrounded the building. Police snipers were quickly positioned on adjacent rooftops. The SAS was also notified of the embassy takeover. By nightfall SAS operators in plainclothes were outside the Iranian embassy, consulting with police officials and assessing the situation.

The British police plan was to drag out the ordeal for as long as possible. For several days, negotiations continued between the terrorist leader—a man known as Oan—and British authorities. But Oan, incensed that his demands were being ignored, killed the Iranian press attaché on May 5 and dumped his body outside the embassy. Oan warned that unless his demands were agreed to immediately, one hostage would be executed on the half hour until everyone inside the building was dead.

This threat broke British tolerance. Prime Minister Margaret Thatcher gave the SAS the green light to end the ordeal. Meanwhile, the British media had gathered to record the events as they unfolded.

PLANNING THE RESCUE

The SAS plan revolved around three four-man teams. Two of the teams would rappel down the rear of the building from the roof. One would stop at the first-floor balcony. The second would go all the way to the ground. The third team would attack from the main road, blasting its way through the main window.

THE RESCUE

The SAS struck at 7:25 P.M. on May 5, just as the sun was setting. The assault from the rear immediately encountered a serious glitch. The teams' rappelling ropes became tangled, preventing the SAS teams from using their explosives to gain entry. A sledgehammer, carried just in case, breached the massive ten-foot-tall windows. Once the windows were shattered open and the ropes untangled, the SAS operators tossed stun grenades into the room.

■ ■

Hearing the blasts and shattering glass, Oan raced to investigate. The police officer being held hostage rushed Oan. The scuffle between the policeman and the terrorist was enough to prevent

An SAS operator storms the Iranian embassy in London during the 1980 hostage rescue.

Oan from shooting at the SAS troopers. Oan was killed by a burst of fire from one of the operators' MP5 submachine guns.

With the assault under way, the SAS team coming in from the front of the building detonated its explosive charges with an immense blast that blew out the main window. Realizing that their time was up, the terrorists began firing their weapons at the hostages. One captive was killed, and a few others were critically wounded.

SAS troopers responded quickly to the bursts of gunfire, racing into the room and engaging the terrorists. Some terrorists had attempted to hide themselves amid the hostages, but the SAS's intelligence helped identify them, and they were killed by the assaulting SAS force. Another terrorist had attempted to leave the building with a group of hostages freed in the assault, but he was identified by SAS personnel and was cut down by an operator's MP5. The last terrorist, wise enough not to resist, was apprehended by the SAS and handed over to Scotland Yard. In all, the assault on Princes Gate took less than five minutes and succeeded in bringing almost all of the hostages to safety.

Operation Nimrod took place in daylight on a London street. Crowds gathered to watch, and TV crews broadcast the operation live around the world.

While the SAS continued to garner a reputation as the best counterterrorism unit, similar units in Italy weren't faring as well. Successes by the Red Brigades, the Communist terrorist organization founded in the 1969, sent a message to the world that Italy was unsafe and unstable.

THE RESCUE OF GENERAL JAMES DOZIER, JANUARY 28, 1982

On December 17, 1981, a Red Brigades team kidnapped Brigadier General James Dozier, the highest-ranking U.S. Army officer assigned to NATO's Southern Command. It was a turning point for Italy's security services. If the general could be located alive and well, then the Red Brigades would forever be humbled.

THE KIDNAPPING

Posing as plumbers, the Red Brigades terrorists knocked on the door of the general's spacious apartment in Verona, Italy. Once inside the flat, they overpowered the general and quietly removed him from the building. The terrorists threw him into a waiting blue van and whisked him to a Red Brigades safe house in Padua, Italy. The kidnappers left no evidence.

FIRST STEPS

Five hours after Dozier's abduction, a communiqué in the name of the Red Brigades was released to the Italian security services. The manhunt had begun.

Hundreds of Italian police officers and secret service agents were dispatched into Italy's urban centers to search for Dozier. On December 27, 1981, the Red Brigades released a photo of the kidnapped general, bruised and looking disoriented, to the news services. The image outraged Italy's leaders and fired up their resolve to locate Dozier, rescue him, and punish his abductors.

Italian police officers search near Verona, Italy, for signs of General Dozier.

The Red Brigades released the image of General Dozier to confirm that he was alive. He holds a poster with Red Brigades' propaganda.

After nearly a month of relentless observation, wiretaps, interrogations of Red Brigades suspects, and other investigative operations, the Italian police came up with a credible tip. They got the address of a possible hideout where Dozier was being held in the city of Padua. A special surveillance team confirmed that Dozier was indeed inside the Padua safe house. NOCS, the state police's elite special operations unit and counterterrorist force, was given the unenviable task of bring Dozier out alive.

PLANNING THE RESCUE

The NOCS section commander, Captain E., faced a difficult assignment. Dozier was a huge catch for the Red Brigades, so he was undoubtedly being held by the best of the group's triggermen. If the operators did not enter the apartment quickly and decisively—or if their movements were discovered before they reached the safe house's front door—Dozier would certainly be killed.

Captain E. opted for a morning hit under the camouflage of honking horns, passing buses, and nearby construction equipment. They'd need the innocent urban noise to disguise their arrival and to get in place for the rescue. The assault would start at 11:30 A.M. on January 28, 1982.

The twelve-member rescue team would wear civilian clothing. Once inside the building, they would produce black masks from their pockets. They would wear bulletproof vests underneath their leather jackets. An additional force of operators, also in civilian dress, would be stationed at a nearby supermarket, just in case a ferocious firefight developed in the building and spread to the street below.

Several blocks away, sitting inside a specially outfitted deployment van, the entry team was briefed with the latest intelligence. The assault team was ready.

NOCS operators outside the Red Brigades safe house in Padua

THE RESCUE

The sounds from the nearby construction site were deafening, as diesel engines and hammering pounded the operators' eardrums. The deployment van circled the neighborhood, moving with the traffic flow, and unloaded the operators in front of the safe house. The twelve men moved inside quickly.

■ ■

Once inside, *the operators placed masks over their heads and produced their weapons from inside their coats. Adrenaline surged through their bodies under the confining body armor. They stopped outside the apartment's door, feeling confident. They heard movement inside but no yelling or signs of a struggle. No shots had been fired. Their cover had not been blown. Dozier was alive!*

It was time to go in. The breacher (or first to enter), a burly member of the squad, kicked down the front door. A second NOCS member followed close behind.

Two Red Brigades terrorists were assigned to guard Dozier. Each had specific orders to execute the prisoner at any sign of trouble. But the NOCS entry team exploded into the apartment with furious speed.

One terrorist was standing still when the operators knocked him unconscious with a karate blow to the forehead. The second terrorist, afforded a few seconds to recover from the shock of the NOCS entry, had managed to unholster his pistol. He was about to aim it at Dozier, who was seated in a corner of the room. But the second NOCS operator, armed with a Beretta M12 submachine gun, swung the weapon like a baseball bat at the terrorist's head and nearly killed him. Dozier had been saved.

■ ■

The rescue of General Dozier was executed without a single shot being fired. Speed, patience, determination, and luck had helped to rescue a man who had become a symbol of Italy under the gun of terrorism and anarchy. Dozier's rescue showed what Italy was determined to become—a nation that would no longer tolerate terrorism.

General Dozier *(right)* smiles soon after his rescue by NOCS operators.

Alberto Fujimori: president of Peru from 1990 to 2000. He was the son of Japanese immigrants and was known for his hard-line rule.

capitalism: an economic system in which private individuals or groups own businesses. Capitalism and Communism are two economic systems typically placed at odds.

Fuerza de Operaciones Especiales (FOE): Peru's special operations force

Movimiento Revolucionario Túpac Amaru (MRTA): a violent Peruvian terrorist group founded in 1983. Túpac Amaru is dedicated to Communism and to undermining Peru's elected government.

Nestor Cerpa Cartolini: leader of the takeover of the Japanese ambassador's house in Lima. He became the head of MRTA after Victor Polay was captured and died in the embassy attack by the FOE.

Victor Polay: Túpac Amaru's top commander who was arrested in 1992 and sentenced to life imprisonment

A Rescue by Peru's FOE

Since the 1980s, the Peruvian government has been fighting against two main Communist rebel groups—the Shining Path and the Movimiento Revolucionario Túpac Amaru (MRTA, or the Túpac Amaru Revolutionary Movement). Both want to replace Peru's capitalist government with a Communist regime.

To combat these threats, the Peruvian government established the Fuerza de Operaciones Especiales (FOE, or Special Operations Force) as its frontline counterterrorist unit. Only the finest soldiers in the Peruvian military were even allowed to consider volunteering for the squad. These operators were not known for their patience. Whether they were raiding a Shining Path jungle hideaway or a MRTA bomb factory, FOE commandos shot first and asked questions later.

Japanese Embassy, Lima, Peru, December 17, 1996–April 22, 1997

MRTA, the smaller of Peru's two terrorist groups, was weakened in the early 1990s by the arrest of its leader, Victor Polay. Some of the remaining MRTA leadership went into hiding. Others struck at Peruvian society and politicians by attacking the Japanese embassy in Lima, the capital, during a cocktail party.

The Hostage Taking

On the night of December 17, 1996, fourteen heavily armed MRTA terrorists stormed the Japanese ambassador's residence in Lima. The terrorists, led by Nestor Cerpa Cartolini, engaged security agents positioned outside the residence with an intense barrage of gun and grenade fire. Within minutes, the MRTA flag was flying from the top of the building.

Inside the Japanese embassy, the terrorists placed explosive charges at all possible entry points. They quickly rounded up the nearly four hundred men and women enjoying the party, including about thirty ambassadors, Peru's foreign and agriculture ministers, six legislators, and the president of the country's supreme court. Alberto Fujimori, the Peruvian president, was not among the guests.

FIRST STEPS

The moment the first shots were fired, police and military units rushed to the ambassador's residence and quickly surrounded the building. The first instinct for local SWAT and military unit commanders was to attack the location, but that could have been a suicidal move.

Before making any moves, the commanders waited for the terrorists to issue their demands. They didn't have to wait long. Unless the Peruvian government released four hundred MRTA prisoners, including the organization's leader Victor Polay, the terrorists would begin killing the hostages. The terrorists also demanded that Peru completely revamp its prison system and that Japan, among the most developed capitalist countries, drastically reduce its role in the Peruvian economy.

Members of the Peruvian police surround the Japanese embassy in Lima, Peru, soon after its takeover by MRTA terrorists.

President Fujimori was of Japanese descent, and the attack symbolically targeted his presidency. The Fujimori government initiated an intense dialogue to end the ordeal peacefully. To show good will toward this process, the terrorists eventually released some 170 women and elderly guests. Meanwhile, the president called in the FOE.

Because so many international diplomats were being held hostage, FOE commanders had to be extremely careful in mounting their rescue. One mistake, and world leaders would be killed. Peruvian negotiators kept the terrorists talking for days and then weeks, while FOE commandos planned an assault no one expected.

PLANNING THE RESCUE

Soon after the ambassador's residence was seized, FOE commanders realized that a sizable force—one larger than FOE could field—would be needed to storm the besieged compound. So the commanders created a 150-man task force of the best army, navy, air force, and police special operations personnel available. They set up a command post and operations center adjacent to the ambassador's residence. From there, they mounted a tenacious psychological warfare campaign that involved routine low-level distractions and disturbances. The noises became so routine that they were expected and not suspected. The objective was to bore the hostage takers so much that they would not notice what was going on around them.

The psychological warfare campaign coincided with a Herculean engineering feat—three tunnels were being dug from the command post to the residence. Explosive charges placed at the mouth of each underground passage would be blown simultaneously, tearing holes through the building's main floor and allowing operators to enter completely by surprise. Half of the assault force would enter the residence from the underground openings. The other half would launch a frontal assault the moment the underground explosions went off.

THE RESCUE

On the afternoon of April 22, 1997, four months after the seizure, the Peruvian commando force was ready. Snipers ringed the residence. Seventy operators prepared for the assault inside the cramped tunnels. Another seventy men awaited the order to rush the compound. Inside the residence, the four months of nothing had made the fourteen terrorists complacent. At just after 3:00 P.M., like they did every day, many of the terrorists put their rifles against a wall and played a game of four-on-four soccer in the living room. Their routine would be fatal.

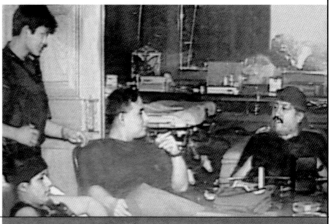

MRTA terrorists take a break during the occupation of the embassy. Nestor Cerpa Cartolini, leader of the terrorists, sits at right.

■ ■

At 3:17 P.M., President Fujimori gave the green light to execute the operation. Within five minutes, the ambassador's main living room and kitchen floors had erupted in a blinding orange fireball and a thick cloud of smoke. The moment the blasts went off, seventy men

Smoke billows out of the embassy after Peruvian special forces set off blasts to gain access.

rushed through the tunnels and seventy men charged the main gate. The Peruvian assault was fast, furious, and designed to be over in a matter of minutes.

The endless stream of men emerging from the holes in the living room and kitchen cut down the terrorists before they could even grab their guns. Other terrorists, hoping to surrender and survive, were reportedly shot at close range. The Peruvian commandos were not interested in taking prisoners. Some of the terrorists managed to put up a fight, but snipers outside and FOE commandos inside decisively overcame their resistance.

■ ■

One of the longest sieges in the history of counterterrorism ended in a twenty-two minute burst of relentless weapons fire. One hostage and two soldiers were killed in the ferocious battle. Twenty-two soldiers and police officers were seriously wounded. All fourteen terrorists were killed.

After the embassy was deemed secure, President Fujimori donned a bulletproof vest and walked among the rubble of the battle-scarred ambassador's residence. He was relieved that the 126-day siege was over. The FOE had answered the threat of terrorism with a masterstroke of imagination and courage.

President Alberto Fujimori *(center in white shirt with vest)* congratulates operators after the rescue of the Japanese embassy.

Alpha Group: first set up during the Soviet period, the counterterrorist unit tasked with operations inside Russia

Chechnya: a breakaway republic within Russia that claimed its independence in 1991. Beginning in 1994, the Russian government sent thousands of Russian troops to the region. A cease-fire was signed in 1996, but the bloody conflict continues.

Federalnaya Sluzhba Bezopasnosti (FSB): the state security organization in Russia. It is the successor to the KGB, which existed during the Soviet period.

fentanyl: an opiate drug first patented in 1963 that is often used in combination with other drugs to anesthetize patients before surgery. In large doses, fentanyl can cause heart and respiratory failure.

Movsar Barayev: the Chechen leader of the terrorists who took over the Moscow theater in 2002

Russia: the largest ex-Soviet republic and the largest country by land in the world

Soviet Union: a large Communist nation in eastern Europe and northern Asia that consisted of fifteen member-republics. It existed from 1922 to 1991.

Special Purpose Islamic Regiment (SPIR): also called Islamic Special Purpose Detachment, a terrorist group with ties to Chechnya

A RESCUE BY RUSSIA'S
ALPHA GROUP

In the aftermath of the 1972 Munich Olympic Massacre, the then Soviet Union set up a special operations unit within its Federanaya Sluzhba Bezopasnosti (FSB, or Federal Security Service). This special ops unit, called Alpha Group, became the country's main counterterrorist and hostage-rescue force.

The FSB had begun as part of the Soviet Union's state security forces. When the Soviet Union fell apart in 1991, long-suppressed ethnic clashes in Russia, the largest of the ex-Soviet republics, came into the open. The FSB was one of the forces tasked with holding these clashes in check. As a result, it became one of the world's busiest counterterrorist units.

Alpha Group's operations in Chechnya, a republic in southwestern Russia seeking independence, were especially extensive in the 1990s. The group executed many raids against Chechen Islamic extremists—acts that further inflamed Chechan resistance.

Chechen rebels celebrate after capturing a Russian tank in 1996.

| THE SIEGE OF A MOSCOW THEATER, OCTOBER 23–26, 2002 | Most Alpha Group members

never believed they'd have to deal with Chechen resistance on the streets of Moscow. In 2002 they found they were wrong, as twenty-two men and nineteen women initiated the most significant act of terrorism ever mounted inside the Russian capital.

THE HOSTAGE TAKING

On the night of October 23, 2002, 850 men, women, and children were sitting inside Moscow's Poshipnikov Zavod Dubrovka Theater watching the second half of *Nord Ost*, a popular musical set during World War II. As intermission was ending, three vans unloaded a force of forty-one heavily armed individuals, all of whom carried assault rifles and handguns. They also wore explosive belts around their waists and carried heavy bombs that were connected to wires and batteries.

The terrorists burst into the theater, firing their weapons in a fusillade of destruction, but the musical's sound system muffled the blasts. Suddenly, several men in camouflage appeared on stage. Male and female terrorists surrounded the audience. The women, in traditional black Muslim veils, carried handguns and explosives. The men, wearing black masks, aimed their weapons at the terrified theatergoers and threatened to shoot everyone in sight.

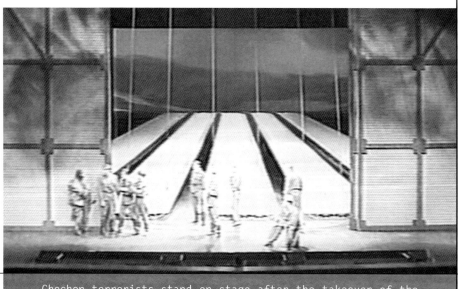

Chechen terrorists stand on stage after the takeover of the Moscow theater in 2002.

As screams turned into panic-stricken pleas for mercy, a young man walked arrogantly to the stage. He introduced himself as Movsar Barayev, the operation's terrorist leader. He declared that unless the Russian military withdrew immediately from war-torn Chechnya, he would order his suicide squad to kill everyone inside the theater and to blow up the building.

Terrified, some theatergoers held their loved ones and wept. Others, using their cellular phones, dialed the police and informed the authorities of their plight. The moment the police heard the name Movsar Barayev, they knew they were in for a troubling ordeal.

FIRST STEPS

Barayev was senior commander of a Chechen group called the Special Purpose Islamic Regiment (SPIR), one of several militant Islamic terrorist groups engaged in the struggle to free Chechnya from Russian rule. The FSB knew what Barayev was capable of. His men had kidnapped and killed foreigners and had mutilated captured Russian troops. Perhaps, most embarrassing for the FSB was the fact that it had declared the young Barayev dead only ten days earlier.

Upon first word of the incident, the FSB mobilized Alpha Group

Movsar Barayev *(seated, right)* is surrounded by other terrorists wearing explosives.

to respond to the challenge. The Alpha unit commanders needed to know how many terrorists there were, what they were armed with, and how many explosive charges they possessed. Several children and some Muslims who had been released were intensively debriefed.

PLANNING THE RESCUE

Negotiations with the terrorists dragged on for forty-eight hours, and there was no sign of the situation ending peacefully. Heavily armed Alpha operators ringed the theater, but no one dared issue the order to mount an attack. It seemed that any entry into the theater would have to be fought for, with firepower and explosives, and that would take time. Even thirty seconds—the time it would take an operator to reach the hostages—would be more than enough for Barayev to order his female operatives to detonate their explosive belts.

For the Alpha commanders, the situation was "lose-lose," regardless of how well trained and determined his men were. It was simply a question of whether they would lose big or lose small.

FSB psychologists were brought into the command post to assess Barayev's mood. They concluded that a religious zealot bent on suicidal vengeance was a foe who could not be negotiated with. The FSB's Chechen experts were also summoned. They concluded that the forty-one terrorists wouldn't release the hostages. They also knew the Russian government would not succumb to extortion.

THE RESCUE

The Russians knew that a frontal assault would end in failure, so a novel idea was kicked around. What about tranquilizing the terrorists to remove them from the equation? The tranquilizer could be a derivative of fentanyl, which can kill pain and cause unconsciousness. But a dose of fentanyl also can shut down a person's breathing and circulation. Nevertheless, the Russians felt they needed to take the risk.

Just after 5:00 A.M. on October 26, 2002, a fine gray mist began to enter the theater. The mist, aerosolized fentanyl, was first heard as a hissing sound. The choking, biting stench of the gas soon followed. The Alpha force was poised to enter the theater the moment the gas was introduced, but before they could make their move, they needed to be absolutely certain that the chemical had knocked out everyone in the theater.

Barayev and his lieutenants knew that the mist was some sort of chemical agent designed to end the ordeal. They ordered the women who were tasked with guarding the hostages to stand fast. The men grabbed their assault rifles and antipersonnel grenades for their final stand. Barayev and his deputies began firing wildly into the night.

But the Russians weren't taking the bait. The Alpha team leaders knew that as long as Barayev was firing at them—and no explosions were heard from inside the auditorium—the hostages still had a chance. Ten minutes after the gas was introduced, movement was still heard in the theater. If the fentanyl was working only on some of the hostages, perhaps, the terrorists were still conscious. There was no more time to wait. Over a secure frequency, the Alpha commander issued the order to move in. The assault was under way.

Barayev and his men put up a fierce but brief fight. The Alpha assault squad braved a wall of fire as they pushed through. After a ten-minute gun battle, all of the twenty-two male terrorists were dead.

The Alpha entry team swarmed into the auditorium, where they heard snoring. Virtually all of the hostages and their women guards were unconscious. The Alpha commandos meticulously scoured the seats in search of the black-clad female terrorists and shot each one at point-blank range. As the hostages were rescued, experts defused the twenty explosive devices spread throughout the theater.

None of the terrorists survived the assault on the theater.

The Alpha rescue operation should have entered the history books as one of the most innovative and courageous ever dared. Faced with a suicidal foe, the Russian commandos had figured out a way to safely storm the location. Not a single Russian operator had been wounded or killed in the assault.

Yet the Russians had not planned for the aftermath of the rescue. Although the standoff had been under way for more than seventy-two hours, the authorities had not mobilized enough medical equipment and personnel to handle the situation. Hostages overcome by the fentanyl were carried outside, with their heads thrown back, as they suffocated or choked. An antidote to the agent was available, but too few medical personnel were on hand to administer it in time. Because of the secrecy that pervaded much of the FSB's work, the authorities didn't tell local hospitals about the fentanyl's use. By the time the explosive devices were defused and the bodies cleared from the theater, 129 hostages had perished

An operator carries out a hostage suffering from the effects of fentanyl gas poisoning.

in the bungled aftermath of a brilliant counterterrorist operation.

EPILOGUE

All of the counterterrorist groups in this book are still active, although their activities are often kept secret. GSG-9, for example, has been involved in the U.S.-led war in Iraq, mostly in protecting personnel and property of the German embassy in Baghdad, the capital of Iraq. In 2004 two GSG-9 operators were killed when their convoy was ambushed by Iraqi rebels. NOCS is working with U.S. security services to develop a better protection program for diplomats and other high-profile personnel stationed in Italy.

The two most recent rescues—in Peru and in Russia—saw developments in the early 2000s. After the embassy rescue in Peru, President Alberto Fujimori continued to run into opposition to his authoritarian rule. Fujimori was declared the winner of the 2000 presidential election, which many Peruvians viewed as fraudulent. Fujimori resigned from office that year while traveling in Japan. By 2004 he was still living in exile there, and the Japanese government had recognized him as a Japanese citizen. The Peruvian government has filed criminal charges against him, which Fujimori continues to deny.

After the Moscow theater rescue, human rights groups initiated discussions about whether the use of the fentanyl-related drug violated the international Chemical Weapons Convention, which regulates the use of chemicals in war or siege situations. In 2003 victims and heirs of victims of the gassing brought lawsuits against the Moscow and Russian governments. A monument to the victims was unveiled in Moscow on the first anniversary of the event. Meanwhile, the Russian government was investigating five alleged accomplices in the theater takeover. ■

*Please note that the information contained in this book was current at the time of publication. To find sources for late-breaking news, please consult the websites listed on pages 68 and 69.

TIMELINE

Israeli	Dutch or German	Peruvian
French	British or Italian	Russian

1831	**French Foreign Legion is created to bring Algeria into the French Empire.**
1922	The Soviet Union is created.
1939-1945	World War II is fought. British Special Air Service (SAS) is established.
1945	Thousands of Jewish Holocaust survivors emigrate to British-controlled Palestine. The United Nations (UN) is founded. South Moluccans side with the Dutch as Indonesia's fight for independence begins.
1948	The State of Israel is declared. The Arabs and Israelis fight one another in 1948 war.
1949	The North Atlantic Treaty Organization (NATO) is established. The Dutch give up their rights to Indonesia. The South Moluccas become part of the state of East Indonesia.
1950	South Moluccans declare themselves independent from Indonesia.
1951	Indonesian forces occupy the South Moluccan Islands.
1954	**Algeria begins its war of independence against France.**
1957	Israel's Sayeret Mat'kal is created.
1961	**The Algerian civil war ends.**
1962	**Algeria wins its independence from France.**
1964	The Palestine Liberation Organization (PLO) is founded.
1967	George Habash forms the Popular Front for the Liberation of Palestine (PFLP).

1968 In Germany the Red Army Faction (RAF) begins its campaign of terror.

1969 The Red Brigades is formed at an Italian university.

1970 Jordanian troops begin an assault on Palestinian refugee camps, an event that comes to be known as Black September.

1971 The PLO forms the Black September Organization.

1972 Sayeret Mat'kal commandos rescue Sabena Airlines passengers from Black September hijackers during Operation Isotope 1. Black September terrorists execute the Munich Olympic Massacre. Germany's Grenzschutzgruppe 9 (GSG-9) is created. The Netherlands' Bijzondere Bijstands Eenheid (BBE) is created.

1973 **Palestinian terrorists seize the Saudi Arabian embassy in Paris, France.**

1974 **France's Groupe d'Intervention de la Gendarmerie Nationale (GIGN) is created.** The Soviet Union establishes the Alpha Group.

1976 **Terrorists from the Front for the Liberation of the Coast of Somalia (FLCS) hijack a school bus in the French Territory of the Afars and Issas. GIGN commandos rescue all but one of the schoolchildren.** PFLP and RAF operatives hijack an Air France plane to Entebbe, Uganda. Sayeret Mat'kal commandos storm the plane and rescue the hostages during Operation Thunderball.

1977 The BBE executes two rescues of hostages—in a school and on a train—taken by a South Moluccan terrorist group. GSG-9 commandos rescue hostages from RAF and Palestinian hijackers in Mogadishu, Somalia, during Operation Magic Fire. **The French Territory of the Afars and Issas becomes independent Djibouti.**

1978 Italy's Nucleo Centrale di Sicurezza (NOCS) is created.

1980   Terrorists of the Democratic Front for the Liberation of Arabistan (DFLA) take over the Iranian embassy in London, England. The SAS carries out Operation Nimrod to rescue the hostages.

1981   The Red Brigades kidnap General James Dozier.

1982   The NOCS rescues General Dozier from the Red Brigades.

1983   **Túpac Amaru Revolutionary Movement (MRTA) forms in Peru.**

1991   The Soviet Union collapses. Chechnya claims its independence from Russia.

1992   **The Groupe Islamique Armé (GIA) is formed. Victor Polay, leader of MRTA, is imprisoned.**

1994   **GIA operatives hijack Air France Flight 8689, which GIGN commandos rescue with all hostages safe.** Russia sends 40,000 troops to Chechnya to subdue a rebellion.

1996   **Túpac Amaru rebels take over the residence in Lima, Peru, of the Japanese ambassador.** Russia signs a cease-fire agreement with Chechnya.

1997   **Peruvian counterterrorist commandos invade the Japanese ambassador's house in Lima, rescuing the hostages held by Túpac Amaru rebels.**

2000   **President Alberto Fujimori of Peru resigns.**

2002   Alpha Group is deployed when Chechen rebels take over a Moscow theater. The rescue results in the accidental deaths of many hostages.

2003   Victims and heirs of victims of the Moscow theater rescue bring lawsuits against the Russian and Moscow governments.

2004   **Fujimori denies allegations of criminal acts while still in exile.**

SELECTED BIBLIOGRAPHY

Bernard, Michael. *GIGN: Le Temps D'un Secret*. Paris: Bibliophile, 2003.

Collin, Richard Oliver, and Gordon L. Freeman. *Winter of Fire: The Abduction of General Dozier and the Downfall of the Red Brigades*. New York: E. P. Dutton, 1990.

Davies, Barry. *Fire Magic: LH181 Hijack to Mogadishu*. London: Bloomsbury Publishing, 1994.

———. *SAS Shadow Warriors of the 21st Century*. Miami: Lewis International, Inc., 2002.

Dobson, Christopher, and Ronald Payne. *Counterattack: The West's Battle against the Terrorists*. New York: Facts on File, 1982.

Gal, Reuven. *Portrait of the Israeli Soldier*. Westport, CT: Greenwood Press, 1986.

Geraghty, Tony. *Who Dares Wins: The Special Air Service—1950 to the Gulf War*. London: Bantam Books, 1992.

Katz, Samuel M. *The Elite*. New York: Pocket Books, 1992.

———. *The Hunt for the Engineer: How Israeli Agents Tracked the Hamas Master Bomber*. New York: Fromm, 1999.

McNab, Andy. *Bravo Two Zero: The True Story of an SAS Patrol behind the Lines in Iraq*. London: Bantam Press, 1993.

Micheletti, Eric. *Le GIGN en Action*. Paris: Histoire et Collections, 1997.

Netanyahu, Iddo. *Entebbe—A Defining Moment in the War on Terrorism—The Jonathan Netanyahu Story*. Green Leaf, AR: New Leaf Press, 2003.

———. *Yoni's Last Battle: The Rescue at Entebbe, 1976*. Jerusalem: Gefen Books, 2001.

Pflug, Jackie Nink. *Miles to Go before I Sleep: My Grateful Journey Back from the Hijacking of Egyptair Flight 648*. Center City, MN: Hazelden Education Materials, 1995.

Tophoven, Rolf. *GSG 9: Kommando Gegen Terrorismus*. Munich: Bernard & Graefe, 1988.

FURTHER READING AND WEBSITES

Books

Baer, Suzie. *Peru's MRTA: Túpac Amaru Revolutionary Movement*. New York: Rosen Publishing Group, 2003.

Corzine, Phyllis. *The Palestinian-Israeli Accord*. San Diego: Lucent Books, 1997.

Currie, Stephen. *Terrorists and Terrorist Groups*. San Diego: Lucent Books, 2002.

Darmon, Peter. *Surprise Attack: Lightning Strikes of the World's Elite Forces*. New York: Barnes & Noble Books, 1993.

Egendorf, Laura K., ed. *Terrorism: Opposing Viewpoints*. San Diego: Greenhaven Press, 2000.

Ferguson, Amanda. *SAS: British Special Air Service*. New York: Rosen Publishing Group, 2003.

Fridell, Ron. *Terrorism: Political Violence at Home and Abroad*. Berkeley Heights, NJ: Enslow Publishers, 2001.

Goldstein, Margaret J. *Israel in Pictures*. Minneapolis: Lerner Publications Company, 2004.

Henderson, Harry. *Global Terrorism: The Complete Reference Guide.* New York: Checkmark Books, 2001.

Hoffman, Bruce. *Inside Terrorism.* New York: Columbia University Press, 1998.

Katz, Samuel M. *Global Counterstrike: International Counterterrorism.* Minneapolis: Lerner Publications Company, 2005.

———. *Jerusalem or Death: Palestinian Terrorism.* Minneapolis: Lerner Publications Company, 2004.

———. *Jihad: Islamic Fundamentalist Terrorism.* Minneapolis: Lerner Publications Company, 2004.

———. *Raging Within: Ideological Terrorism.* Minneapolis: Lerner Publications Company, 2004.

Midgley, Ruth, ed. *Eyewitness Visual Dictionaries: Special Military Forces.* New York: Dorling Kindersley, 1993.

Netanyahu, Benjamin. *Fighting Terrorism: How Democracies Can Defeat the International Terrorist Network.* New York: Farrar, Straus and Giroux, 2001.

Websites

BBC News World Edition
<http://news.bbc.co.uk/>
The website of the British Broadcasting Corporation provides extensive coverage of international news, as well as country profiles and in-depth reports on terrorist issues.

The Center for Defense Information: Terrorism Project
<http://www.cdi.org/terrorism>
This site provides detailed articles on a variety of topics related to terrorism.

CNN.com
<http://www.cnn.com>
This news site is a source of breaking news on terrorism and other world events. It also offers a searchable archive of past articles.

Economist.com
<http://www.economist.com>
Regularly updated, this online version of the *Economist* magazine offers up-to-date economic information, as well as commentary on how terrorist activities affect local and world economies.

The New York Times on the Web
<http://www.nytimes.com>
This online version of the newspaper offers both up-to-date and archived articles on the major terrorist groups.

Terrorism Questions and Answers
<http://www.terrorismanswers.com>
This site, operated by the Markle Foundation (a nonprofit group that studies communications and media), presents a wealth of information through question-and-answer sheets on various aspects of terrorism.

The Terrorism Research Center
<http://www.terrorism.com>
In addition to its historic information on terrorist groups, this site also provides antiterrorist information and links to other useful sites.

Terrorist Group Profiles
<http://library.nps.navy.mil/home/tgp/tgp2.htm>
This website is run by the Dudley Knox Library at the U.S. Naval Postgraduate School in Monterey, California. It features profiles of terrorist groups, chronologies of terrorist incidents, and a link to the U.S. State Department.

This Is Baader-Meinhof
<http://www.baader-meinhof.com>
This website provides a timeline of Red Army Faction activities, a who's who, a guide to terminology, and more.

Time Online Edition
<http://www.time.com/time>
This online version of the magazine can be searched by specific continents as well as in general.

U.S. Department of State Counterterrorism Office
<http://www.state.gov/s/ct>
The U.S. government maintains this site, which offers information on historic and active terrorist groups.

INDEX

ABOUT THE AUTHOR

Samuel M. Katz is an expert in the fields of international terrorism and counterterrorism, military special operations, and law enforcement. He has written more than twenty books and dozens of articles on these subjects. He is the editor in chief of *Special Operations Report* (www.specialoperationsreport.com). He has also created documentary films and lectured to law-enforcement and counterterrorist agencies around the world. The Terrorist Dossiers series is his first foray into the field of nonfiction for young people.

PHOTO ACKNOWLEDGMENTS

The images in this book are used with the permission of: © Samuel M. Katz, p. 5, 35; Pridan Moshe/State of Israel National Photo Collection, p. 8; © Hulton Archive/Getty Images, pp. 9, 45; Milner Moshe/State of Israel National Photo Collection, p. 10; Cohen Fritz/State of Israel National Photo Collection, p. 11; IDF Spokesperson/courtesy Samuel M. Katz, pp. 12, 20; Ron Ilan/State of Israel National Photo Collection, p. 13; © Bettmann/CORBIS, pp. 14, 21, 46, 48, 49; State of Israel National Photo Collection, p. 17; Herman Chanania/State of Israel National Photo Collection, p. 18; SIRPA Gendarmerie/courtesy Samuel M. Katz, p. 26; © Parrot Pascal/CORBIS SYGMA, p. 28; © Le Segretain Pascal/CORBIS SYGMA, p. 29; © ORBAN/CORBIS SYGMA, p. 30; © Gabriel Bouys/AFP/Getty Images, p. 31; Royal Netherlands Marine Corps/courtesy Samuel M. Katz, pp. 34, 36; AP/Wide World Photos, pp. 37, 44, 52, 54 (top), 57, 62; © UPI/CORBIS, pp. 38, 47; © Robin Adshead/The Military Picture Library/CORBIS, p. 42; © CORBIS SYGMA, pp. 54 (bottom), 55; © Getty Images, p. 58; © AFP/Getty Images, pp. 59, 61. Maps on pp. 16 and 25 by Laura Westlund. Cover image © CORBIS SYGMA.